HAL LEONARD
GUITAR METHOD

GUITAR FOR KIDS
METHOD & SONGBOOK

BY BOB MORRIS &
JEFF SCHROEDL

P9-APJ-878

ISBN 978-1-4234-8902-3

HAL•LEONARD®
CORPORATION
7777 W. BLUEMOUND RD. P.O. BOX 13819 MILWAUKEE, WI 53213

Visit Hal Leonard Online at
www.halleonard.com

METHOD CONTENTS

SONGBOOK CONTENTS

SELECTING YOUR GUITAR

Guitars come in three different sizes:

Guitars also come in three basic types:

Full size   3/4 size   1/2 size   Electric   Acoustic   Classical

Electric guitars are thinner and usually easier for beginners to hold. Acoustic guitars have a clean, bright sound and are portable. Classical guitars have nylon strings which are often easier on the fingers. Choose a guitar that best fits you.

Too Big   Good Fit

PARTS OF THE GUITAR

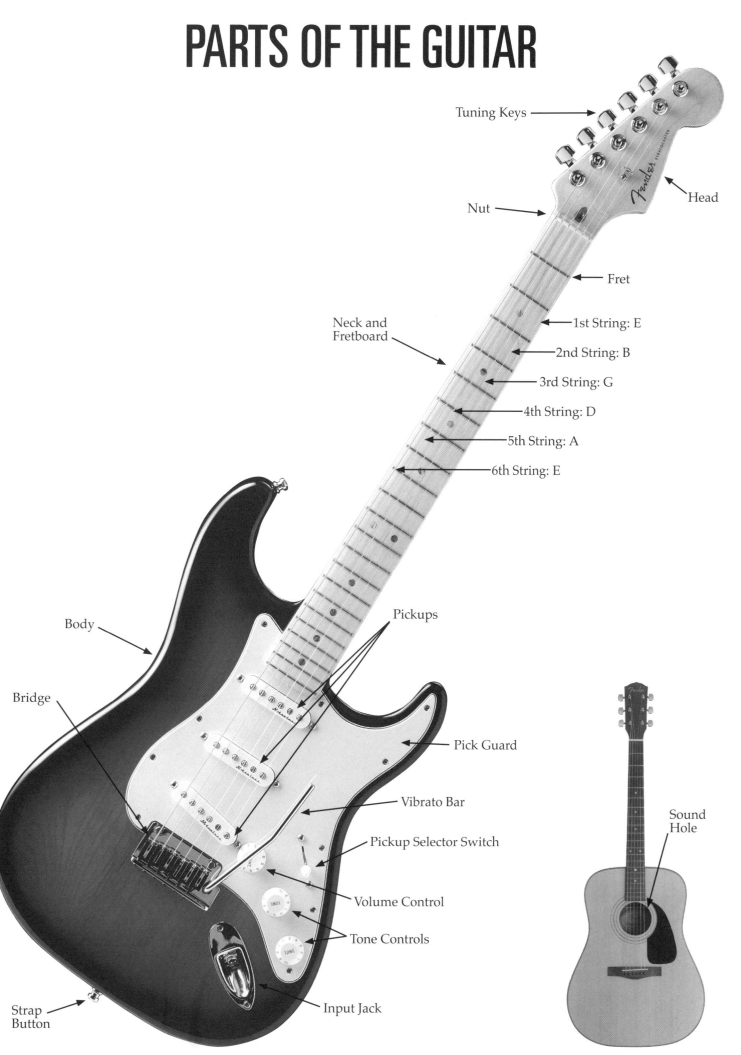

Tuning Keys

Head

Nut

Fret

Neck and Fretboard

1st String: E

2nd String: B

3rd String: G

4th String: D

5th String: A

6th String: E

Pickups

Body

Pick Guard

Bridge

Vibrato Bar

Pickup Selector Switch

Volume Control

Tone Controls

Input Jack

Strap Button

Sound Hole

HOLDING THE GUITAR

- Sit up straight and relax

- Place your feet flat on the floor or place one foot on a foot stool

- Tilt the neck of the guitar slightly upwards

- Raise your thigh to prevent the guitar from slipping; adjust chair or foot stool

- Look at the photos below and match the body position

HAND POSITION

Left Hand

Fingers are numbered 1 through 4.
Press the string firmly between the frets.

Place your thumb in the middle of the back of
the neck. Arch your fingers and keep your palm
clear of the neck.

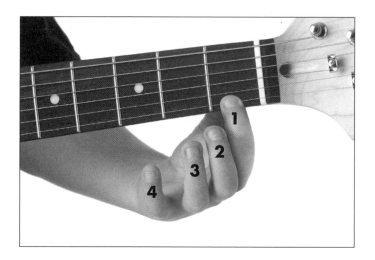

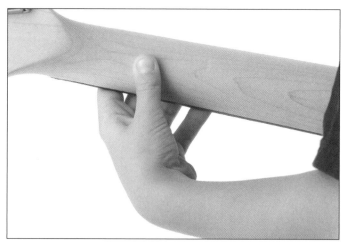

Right Hand

Hold the pick between your thumb and
index finger.

Pluck the string with a downward motion of
the pick or thumb halfway between the bridge
and neck.

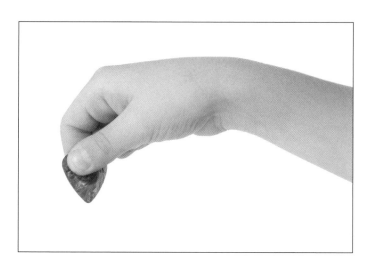

THE C CHORD

A **chord** is sounded when more than two strings are played at the same time. To play your first chord, C, use your 1st finger to press the 2nd string at the 1st fret.

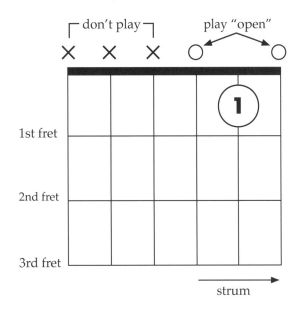

Music has a steady **beat,** like the ticking of a clock. Count aloud as you strum.

strum	strum	strum	strum	strum	strum	strum	strum
∕	∕	∕	∕	∕	∕	∕	∕
1	2	3	4	1	2	3	4

ARE YOU STRUMMING?  TRACK 1

C

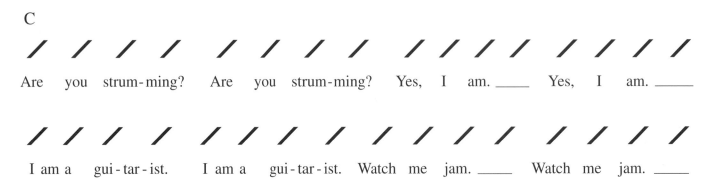

∕ ∕ ∕ ∕   ∕ ∕ ∕ ∕   ∕ ∕ ∕ ∕   ∕ ∕ ∕ ∕

Are you strum-ming? Are you strum-ming? Yes, I am. ____ Yes, I am. ____

∕ ∕ ∕ ∕   ∕ ∕ ∕ ∕   ∕ ∕ ∕ ∕   ∕ ∕ ∕ ∕

I am a gui-tar-ist. I am a gui-tar-ist. Watch me jam. ____ Watch me jam. ____

TEACHER MELODY:

THE G7 CHORD

Use your 1st finger to press the 1st string at the 1st fret.

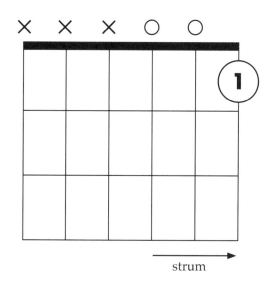

strum

Bar lines divide music into **measures**.   A **double bar line** means the end.

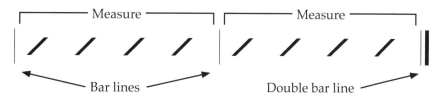

Measure   Measure

Bar lines   Double bar line

COCONUT  TRACK 2

Words and Music by
Harry Nilsson

G7

Put the lime in the coco - nut, drink 'em both up. Put the lime in the coco-nut, drink 'em both up.

Doc - tor,   is there   nothing I can take?   Doc - tor,   to relieve this belly ache?

TEACHER MELODY:

CHANGING CHORDS

Practice strumming the C chord, and then move to G7.

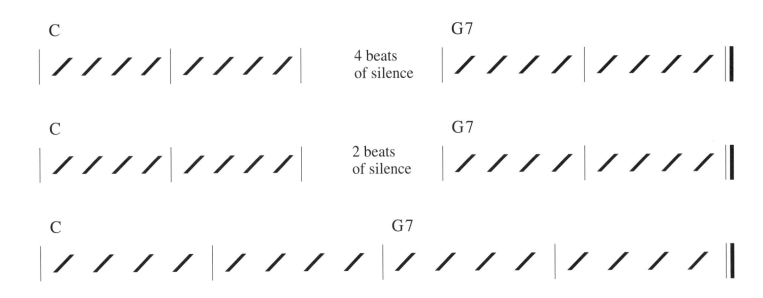

YELLOW SUBMARINE

Words and Music by John Lennon
and Paul McCartney

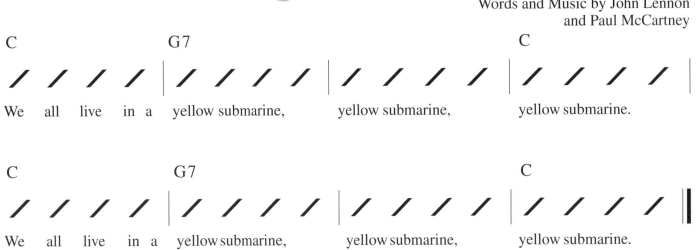

TEACHER MELODY:

THE HOKEY POKEY

 TRACK 4

Words and Music by Charles P. Macak,
Tafft Baker and Larry LaPrise

C

You put your right foot in, you put your right foot out. You put your

G7

right foot in, and you shake it all about. You

do the Hokey Pokey and you turn yourself around.

C

That's what it's all a - bout.

Repeat sign
(Play again from the beginning)

Additional Lyrics

Left foot
Right arm
Left arm
Whole self

TEACHER MELODY:

THE E MINOR CHORD

Use your 2nd finger to press the 4th string at the 2nd fret.

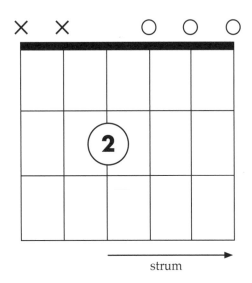

strum

GET UP STAND UP

TRACK 5

Words and Music by Bob Marley
and Peter Tosh

Em

Get up,   stand up.   Stand up for   your right.

Get up,   stand up.   Don't give up   the fight.

TEACHER MELODY:

ELEANOR RIGBY

 TRACK 6

Words and Music by John Lennon
and Paul McCartney

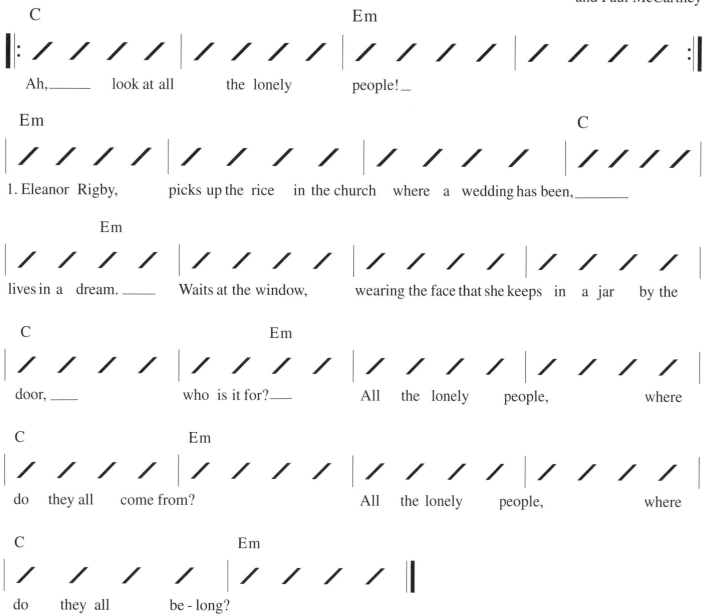

C   **Em**

Ah,_____ look at all the lonely people!_

Em   **C**

1. Eleanor Rigby, picks up the rice in the church where a wedding has been,_____

Em

lives in a dream._____ Waits at the window, wearing the face that she keeps in a jar by the

C   **Em**

door,_____ who is it for?____ All the lonely people, where

C   **Em**

do they all come from? All the lonely people, where

C   **Em**

do they all be - long?

TEACHER MELODY:

THE NOTE E

So far, you have learned to play chords. If you remember, a chord is sounded when more than two strings are played together. Now let's play some single notes.

To play the note E, pluck the 1st string open using a downward motion of the thumb or pick.

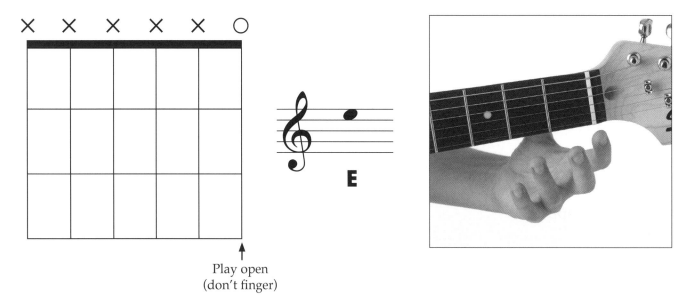

Play open
(don't finger)

Music is written on a **staff** of five lines and four spaces. Each line and space of a staff has a letter name. A **clef** appears at the beginning of every staff. Guitar music is written using the **treble clef**.

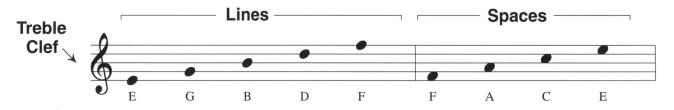

The open 1st string is the note E in the top space of the staff. Play each E note slowly and evenly, using a downward motion of the thumb or pick.

MALAGUEÑA TRACK 7

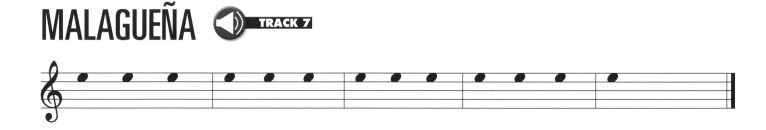

TEACHER ACCOMPANIMENT:

14

THE NOTE F

Use your 1st finger to press the 1st string at the 1st fret.

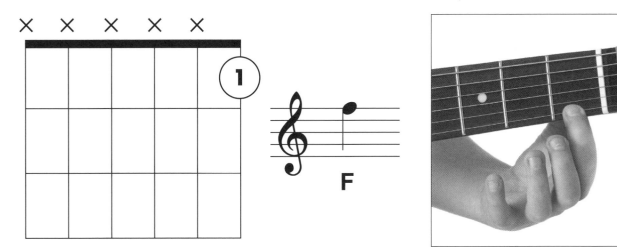

A **time signature** appears at the beginning of a piece of music. It tells how many beats are in each measure and what kind of note gets one beat. In 4/4 ("four-four") time, there are four beats in each measure and the **quarter note** gets one beat. A solid note with a stem (♩) is called a quarter note.

TWO NOTE TUNE TRACK 8

Time Signature

TEACHER ACCOMPANIMENT:

HAMMER HEAD TRACK 9

TEACHER ACCOMPANIMENT:

THE NOTE G

Use your 3rd finger to press the 1st string at the 3rd fret.

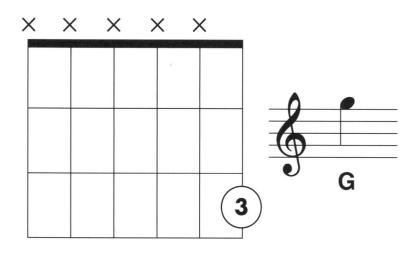

A **half note** (𝅗𝅥) lasts two beats. It is twice as long as a quarter note (𝅘𝅥).

SECRET AGENT TRACK 10

Count: 1 - 2   3   4

TEACHER ACCOMPANIMENT:

GEE WHIZ TRACK 11

Count: 1   2   3 - 4

TEACHER ACCOMPANIMENT:

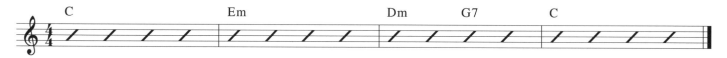

THE NOTE B

Now let's move to the 2nd string. To play the note B, pluck the 2nd string open.

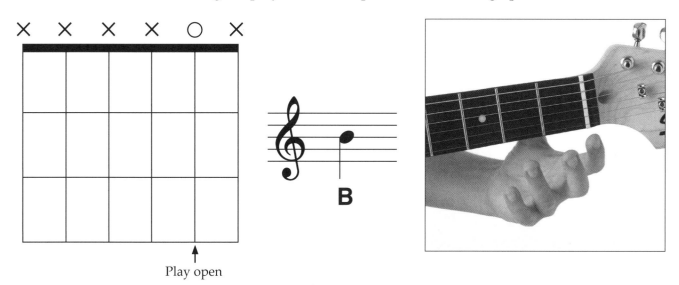

Play open

A **whole note** (𝅝) lasts four beats. It is as long as four quarter notes or two half notes.

COOL BLUES  TRACK 12

Count: 1 2 3 4   1 - 2 - 3 - 4

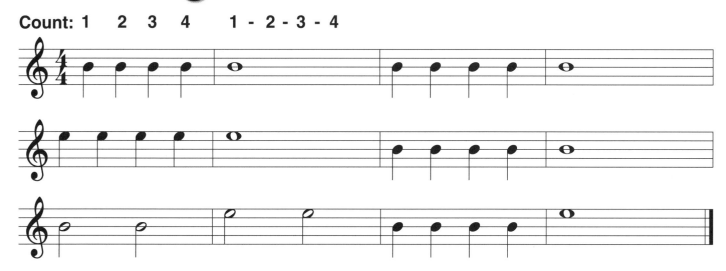

TEACHER ACCOMPANIMENT:

Moderate Shuffle (♫ = ♩♪)

17

THE NOTE C

Use your 1st finger to press the 2nd string at the 1st fret.

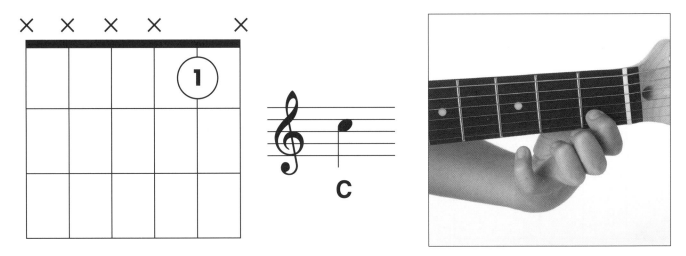

Rests are sounds of silence. The **quarter note rest** (𝄽) means to be silent for one beat.

DOUBLE TROUBLE

TEACHER ACCOMPANIMENT:

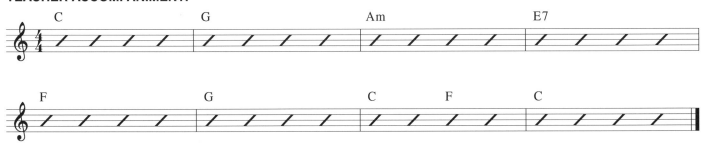

THE NOTE D

Use your 3rd finger to press the 2nd string at the 3rd fret.

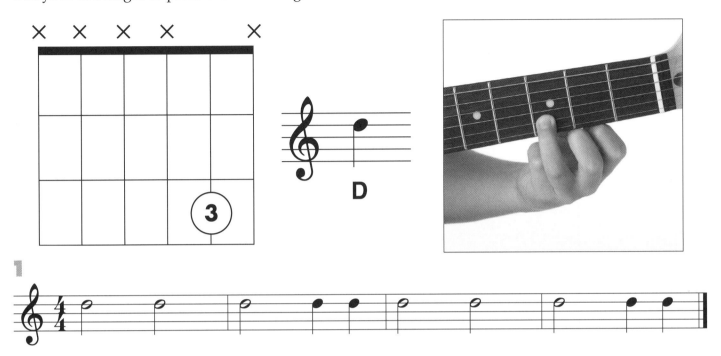

1

The **half note rest** (▬) means to be silent for two beats.

2

ROCK CLIMBING   TRACK 14

TEACHER ACCOMPANIMENT:

NOTE REVIEW

You have learned six notes now: three on the 1st string and three on the 2nd string.

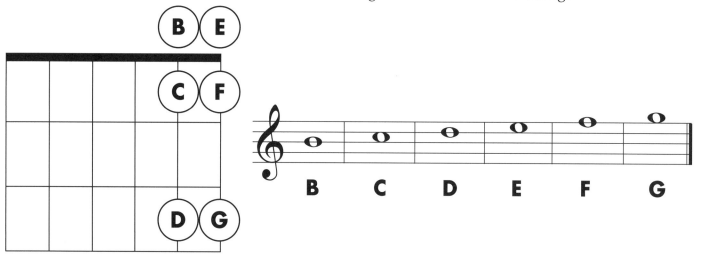

The notes in the following exercises move from string to string. As you are playing one note, look ahead to the next and get your fingers in position.

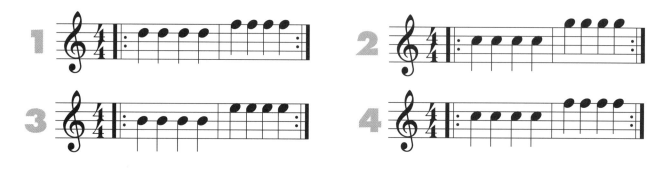

ODE TO JOY   TRACK 15

Beethoven

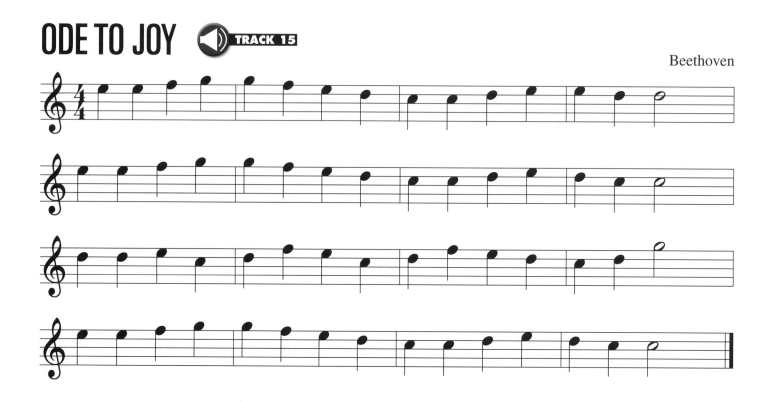

Some songs begin with **pickup notes**. Count the missing beats out loud before you start playing.

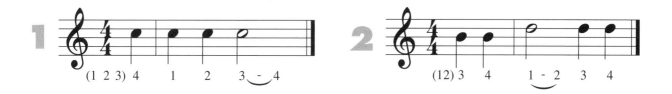

ROCK & ROLL — PART II (THE HEY SONG)

Words and Music by Mike Leander
and Gary Glitter

THE G CHORD

Use your 3rd finger to press the 1st string at the 3rd fret.

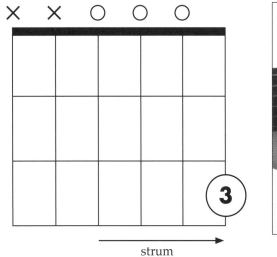

strum

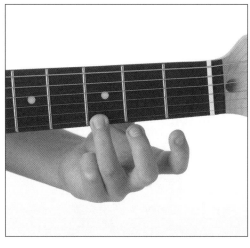

Strum marks are sometimes written on the staff to help you keep track of where the strums are within the measure.

ABC
TRACK 17

Words and Music by Alphonso Mizell,
Frederick Perren, Deke Richards and Berry Gordy

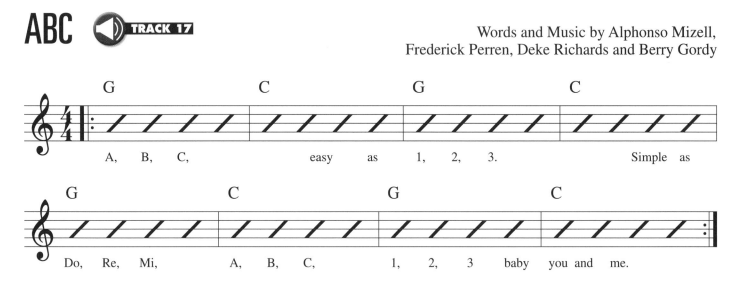

A, B, C,   easy as 1, 2, 3.   Simple as

Do, Re, Mi,   A, B, C,   1, 2, 3 baby you and me.

TEACHER MELODY:

THE D CHORD

For the D chord, you will need to press three notes at the same time.

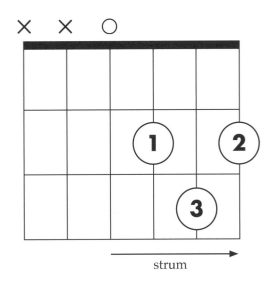

strum

LAND OF A THOUSAND DANCES

Words and Music by
Chris Kenner

Na,   na,na,na,na,   na,na,na,na,   na, na, na,   na,na,   na,   na,na,na,na.

TEACHER MELODY:

CHORD TO CHORD

You can now play five different chords. Let's practice changing between two chords at a time.
Go slow at first; it's okay to pause between chords if you need to in the beginning.

THIS LAND IS YOUR LAND

Words and Music by
Woody Guthrie

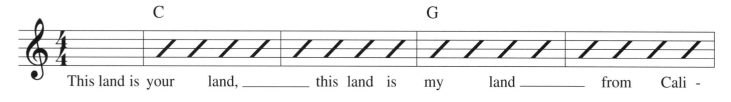

This land is your   land, _____ this land is   my   land _____ from Cali -

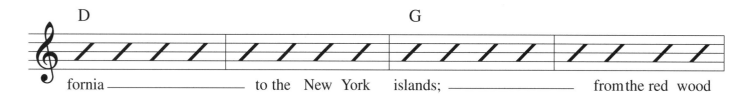

fornia _____ to the New York   islands; _____ from the red wood

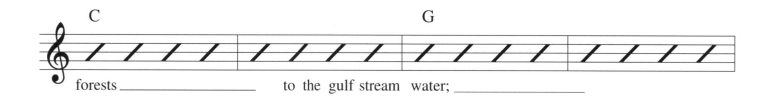

forests _____ to the gulf stream water; _____

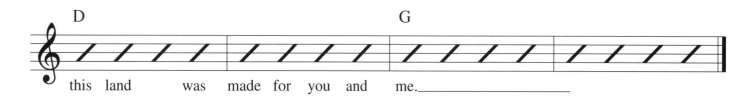

this land   was   made for   you   and   me._____

TEACHER MELODY:

YOU ARE MY SUNSHINE  TRACK 20

Words and Music by
Jimmie Davis

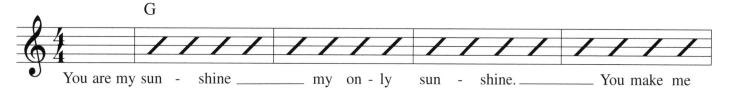

You are my sun - shine _____ my on - ly sun - shine. _____ You make me

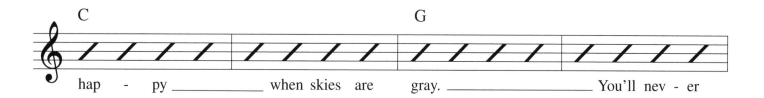

hap - py _____ when skies are gray. _____ You'll nev - er

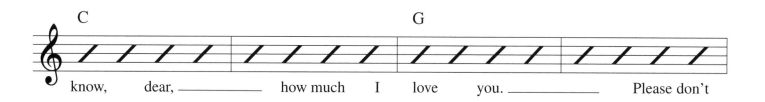

know, dear, _____ how much I love you. _____ Please don't

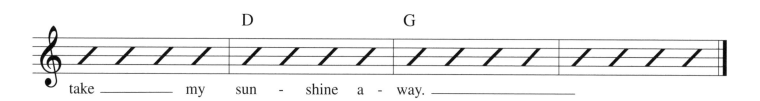

take _____ my sun - shine a - way. _____

TEACHER MELODY:

So far, you have played four downstrums for each measure. Now let's strum twice for every beat, or eight times for each measure. Alternate between downstrums and upstrums.

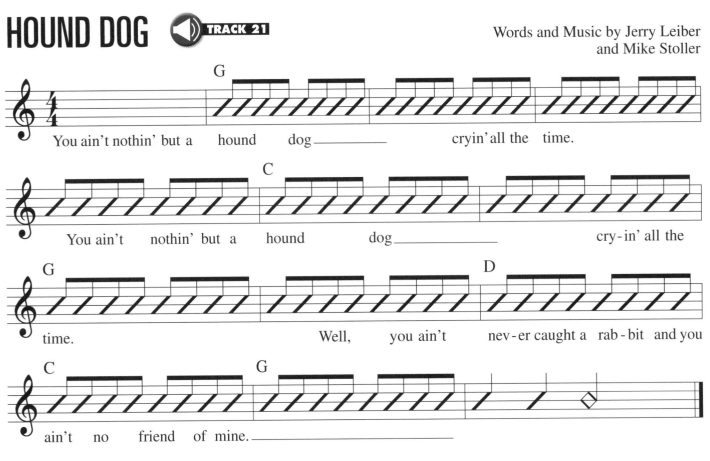

down   up   down   up   down   up   down   up

Try the new down-up strum with songs you learned earlier, and then try "Hound Dog."

HOUND DOG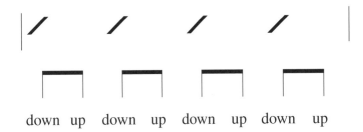

Words and Music by Jerry Leiber
and Mike Stoller

G

You ain't nothin' but a   hound   dog_____   cryin' all the   time.

C

You ain't   nothin' but a   hound   dog_____   cry-in' all the

G   D

time.   Well,   you ain't   nev-er caught a rab-bit and you

C   G

ain't   no   friend   of mine._____

TEACHER MELODY:

BROWN EYED GIRL

 TRACK 22

This famous song by Van Morrison uses four chords. You can strum with all downstrokes or use the new down-up pattern.

Words and Music by
Van Morrison

Intro

G   C   G   D

Verse

G   C   G   D

Hey, where did we go?
laughing and a-running, hey, hey,

Days when the rains came,
skipping and a - jumping.

G   C   G   D

down in the hollow
In the misty morning fog with

playin' a new game,
our heart's a-thumping, and

C   D   G   Em   C   D

you, my brown eyed girl.

You, my brown eyed

G   D

girl.

Do you remember when we used to sing:

Chorus

G   C   G   D

sha la la la la la la la la la la te da.

G   C   G   D   G

Sha la la la la la la la la la la te da, la te da.

TEACHER MELODY:

Intro   G   C   G   D   **Verse** G   C

etc.

THE NOTES G & A

You already learned how to play the note G on the 1st string. Another note G can be played by plucking the 3rd string open. To play the note A, press the 3rd string at the 2nd fret.

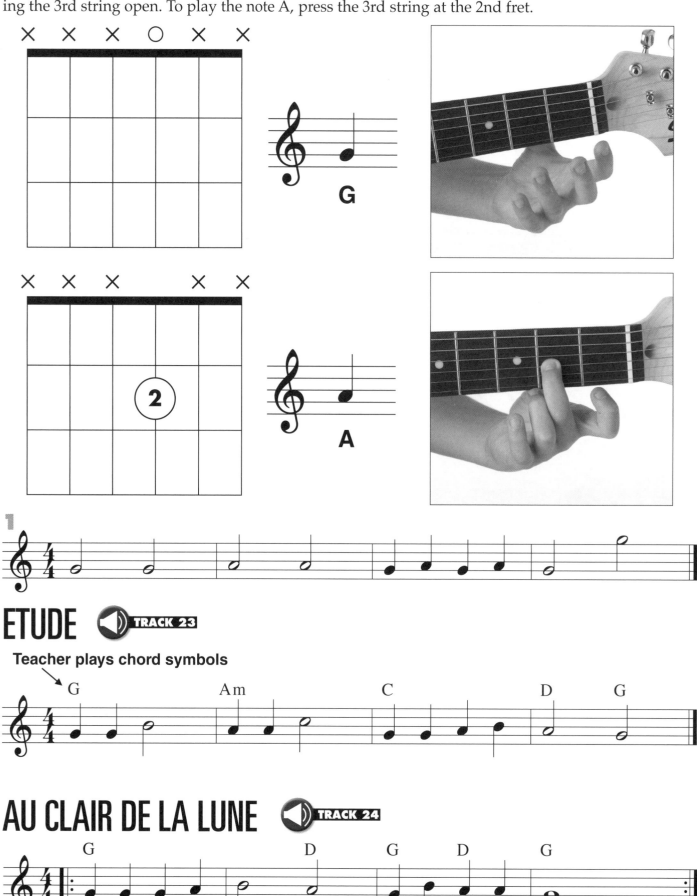

1

ETUDE TRACK 23

Teacher plays chord symbols

G   Am   C   D   G

AU CLAIR DE LA LUNE TRACK 24

G   D   G   D   G

LOVE ME TENDER  TRACK 25

Words and Music by Elvis Presley
and Vera Matson

Teacher plays chord symbols

Love me ten - der, love me sweet; nev - er let me go.

You have made my life com - plete, and I love you so.

Love me ten - der, love me true, all my dreams ful - fill.

For my dar - lin' I love you, and I al - ways will.

THREE-FOUR TIME

Some music has three beats per measure instead of four. The symbol for three-four time is:

 Three beats per measure; quarter note (♩) gets one beat.

BIRTHDAY SONG  TRACK 26

Teacher plays chord symbols →

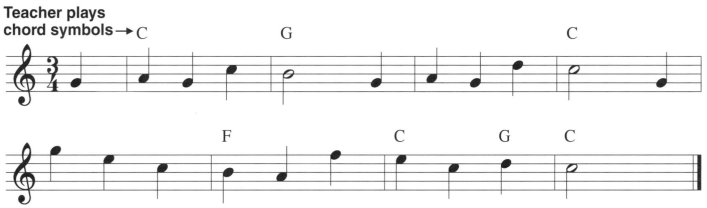

THE A CHORD

Use your 1st, 2nd, and 3rd fingers to press the 4th, 3rd, and 2nd strings at the 2nd fret. Arch your fingers so the 1st string rings open.

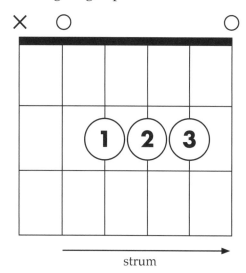

strum

LOW RIDER

 TRACK 27

Words and Music by Sylvester Allen, Harold R. Brown, Morris Dickerson, Jerry Goldstein, Leroy Jordan, Lee Oskar, Charles W. Miller and Howard Scott

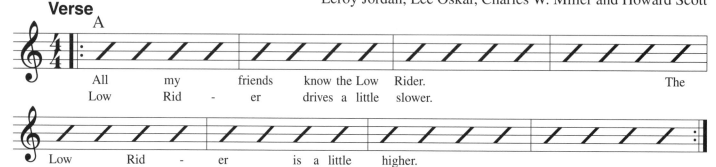

All   my   friends   know the Low   Rider.   The
Low   Rid   -   er   drives a little slower.

Low   Rid   -   er   is a little   higher.
Low   Rid   -   er,   he's a real   go - er.

Take a little trip,   take a little trip,   take a little trip   and see.

TEACHER MELODY:

SURFIN' U.S.A.

TRACK 28

Strum along with this famous Beach Boys song.

Words and Music by
Chuck Berry

whole rest

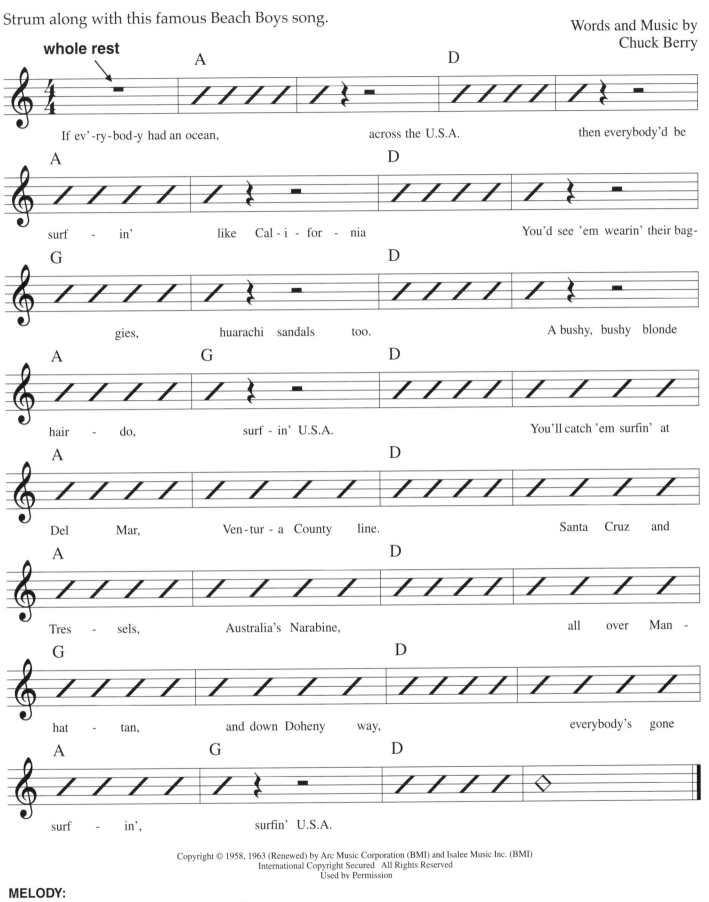

A   D

If ev'-ry-bod-y had an ocean,   across the U.S.A.   then everybody'd be

A   D

surf - in'   like Cal - i - for - nia   You'd see 'em wearin' their bag-

G   D

gies,   huarachi sandals too.   A bushy, bushy blonde

A   G   D

hair - do,   surf - in' U.S.A.   You'll catch 'em surfin' at

A   D

Del   Mar,   Ven - tur - a County line.   Santa Cruz and

A   D

Tres - sels,   Australia's Narabine,   all over Man -

G   D

hat - tan,   and down Doheny way,   everybody's gone

A   G   D

surf - in',   surfin' U.S.A.

MELODY:

A

If ev- 'ry-bod-y had an   o - cean.... _   **etc.**

You now know enough about the guitar to play either the notes or the chords for this final song!

I'M A BELIEVER

Words and Music by
Neil Diamond

Intro

Verse

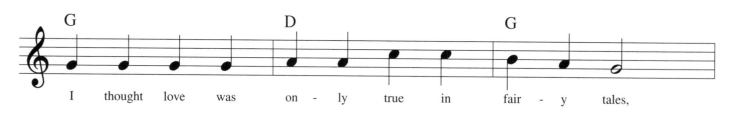

I thought love was on - ly true in fair - y tales,

meant for some - one else but not for

Pre-Chorus

me.   Love was out to

get me.   That's the way it seemed.

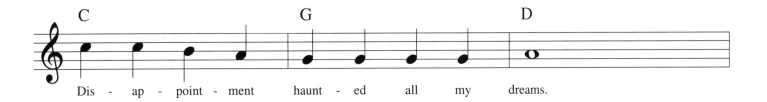

Dis - ap - point - ment haunt - ed all my dreams.

Chorus

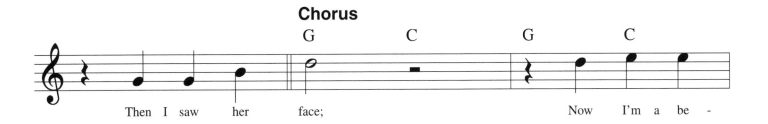

Then I saw her face; Now I'm a be -

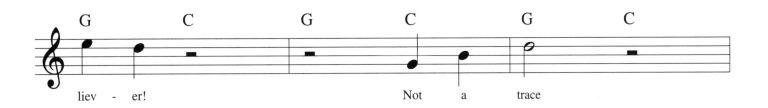

liev - er! Not a trace

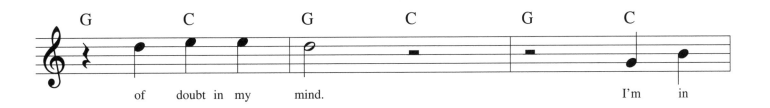

of doubt in my mind. I'm in

love, I'm a be - liev - er! I couldn't

leave her if I tried.

CERTIFICATE OF ACHIEVEMENT

Congratulations to

_____

(YOUR NAME)

_____

(DATE)

You have completed

GUITAR FOR KIDS

_____

(TEACHER SIGNATURE)

You are now ready for

HAL LEONARD GUITAR METHOD BOOK 1

GUITAR FOR KIDS SONGBOOK

PAPERBACK WRITER

Words and Music by John Lennon
and Paul McCartney

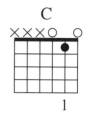

Verse

G7

Dear Sir or Madam, will you read my book? It took me years to write, will you
dirt - y story of a dirt - y man, and his cling - ing wife doesn't

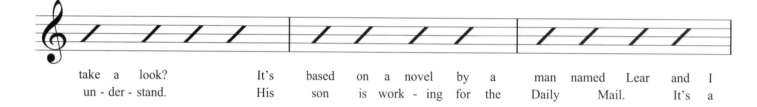

take a look? It's based on a novel by a man named Lear and I
un - der - stand. His son is work - ing for the Daily Mail. It's a

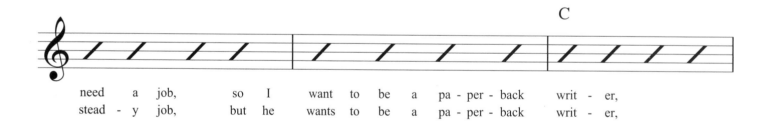

C

need a job, so I want to be a pa - per - back writ - er,
stead - y job, but he wants to be a pa - per - back writ - er,

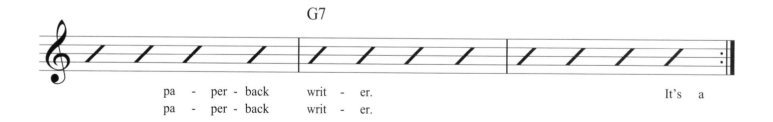

G7

pa - per - back writ - er. It's a
pa - per - back writ - er.

Outro

G7

Pa - per - back writ - er.

DON'T WORRY, BE HAPPY

Words and Music by
Bobby McFerrin

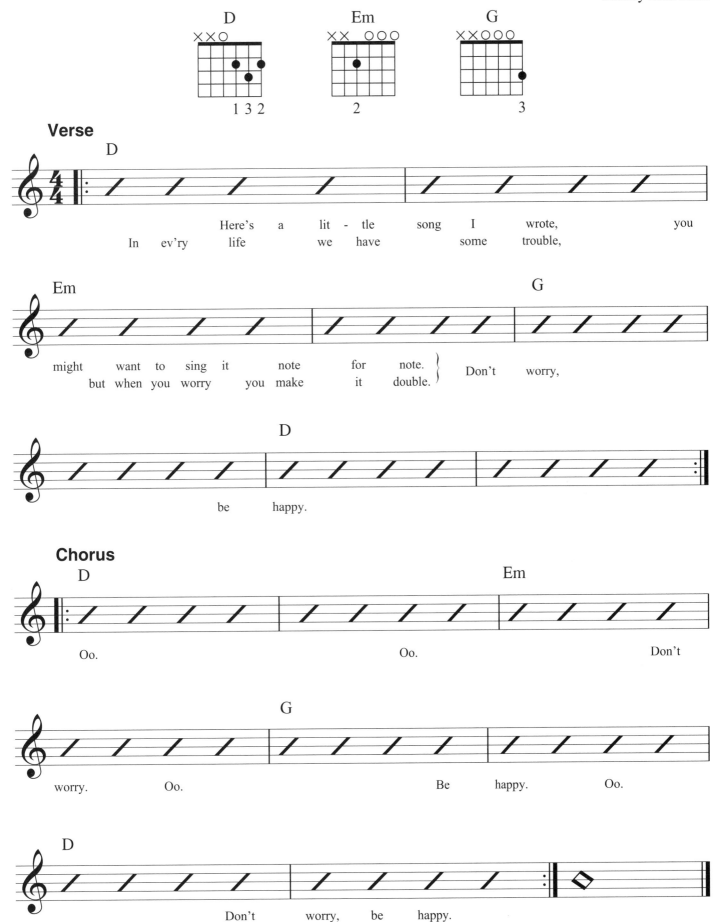

FEELIN' ALRIGHT

Words and Music by
Dave Mason

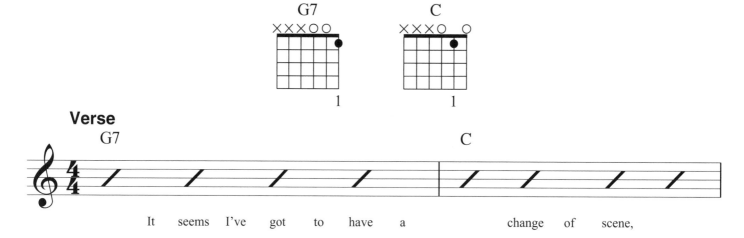

Verse

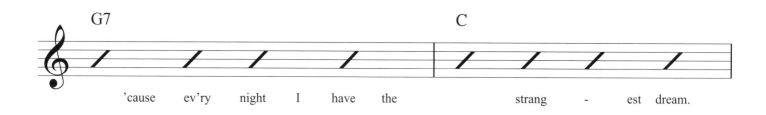

It seems I've got to have a change of scene,

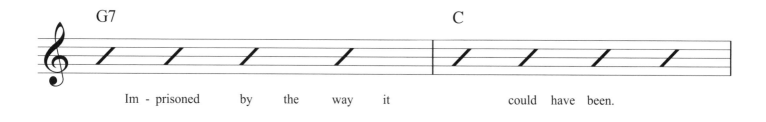

'cause ev'ry night I have the strang - est dream.

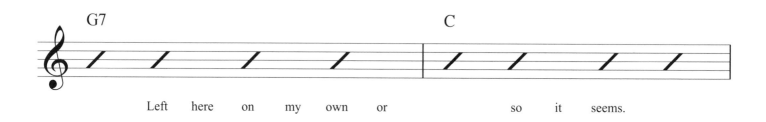

Im - prisoned by the way it could have been.

Left here on my own or so it seems.

I've got to leave be - 'fore I start to scream,

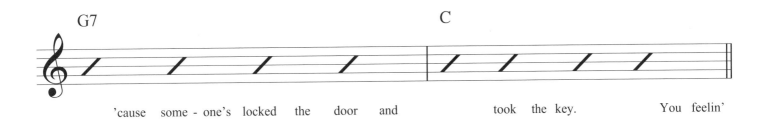

'cause some-one's locked the door and took the key. You feelin'

Chorus

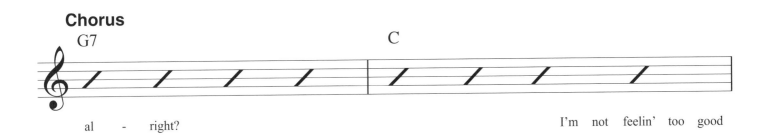

al - right? I'm not feelin' too good

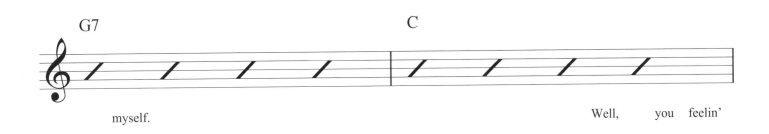

myself. Well, you feelin'

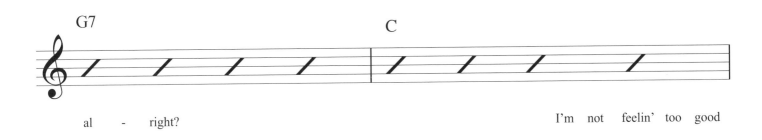

al - right? I'm not feelin' too good

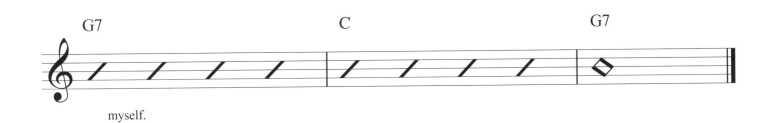

myself.

JAMBALAYA (ON THE BAYOU)

Words and Music by
Hank Williams

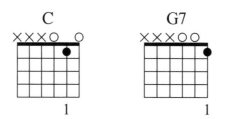

Verse

Good - bye, Joe, me gotta go, me oh

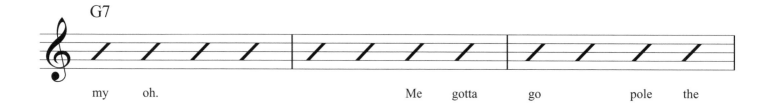

my oh. Me gotta go pole the

pirogue down the bayou. My Y -

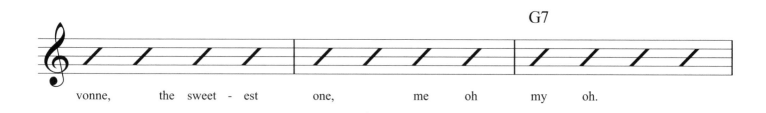

vonne, the sweet - est one, me oh my oh.

Son of a gun, we'll have big fun on the

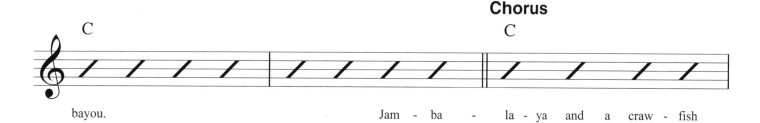

C   C

bayou.   Jam - ba - la - ya   and   a   craw - fish

G7

pie   and fillet   gumbo.   'Cause to -

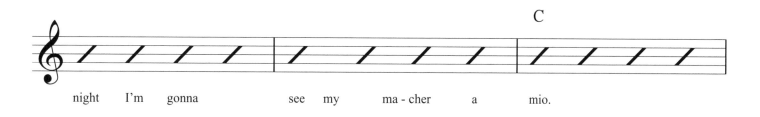

C

night   I'm   gonna   see   my   ma - cher   a   mio.

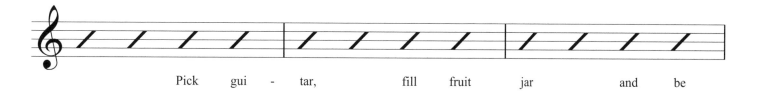

Pick   gui - tar,   fill   fruit   jar   and   be

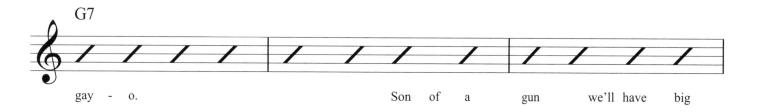

G7

gay - o.   Son   of   a   gun   we'll   have   big

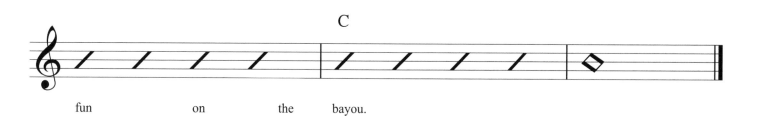

C

fun   on   the   bayou.

ELECTRIC AVENUE

Words and Music by
Eddy Grant

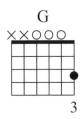

Verse

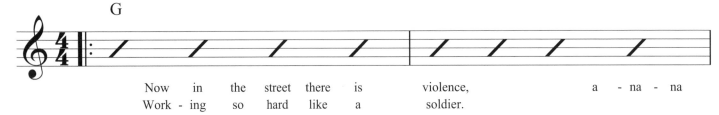

Now   in   the   street   there   is   violence,   a - na - na
Work - ing   so   hard   like   a   soldier.

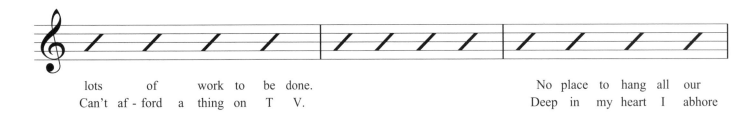

lots   of   work   to   be   done.   No place   to   hang   all   our
Can't af - ford   a   thing   on   T   V.   Deep   in   my   heart   I   abhore

washing,   I   na - na   can't   blame   it   all   on   the   sun.
ya.   Can't   get   food   for   the   kid.

Chorus

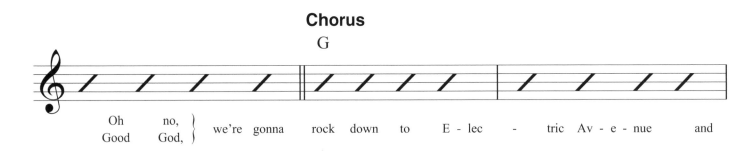

Oh   no,   }   we're   gonna   rock   down   to   E - lec   -   tric   Av - e - nue   and
Good   God, }

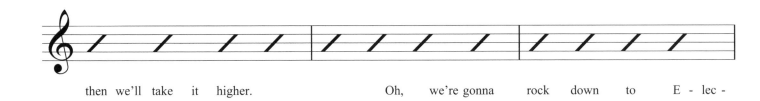

then   we'll   take   it   higher.   Oh,   we're   gonna   rock   down   to   E - lec -

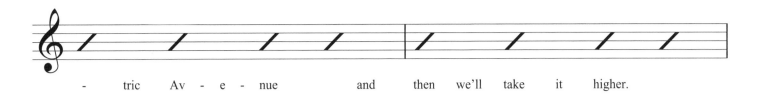

- tric Av - e - nue   and   then   we'll   take   it   higher.

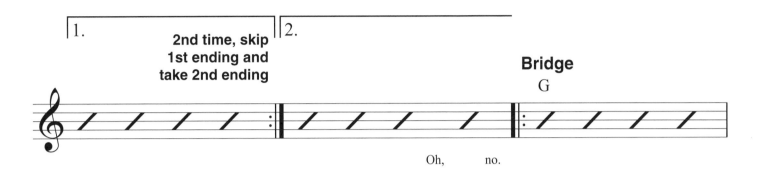

1.

**2nd time, skip
1st ending and
take 2nd ending**

2.

Bridge
G

Oh,   no.

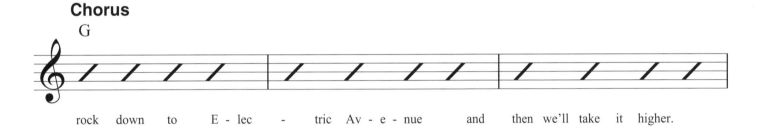

Play 3 times

Oh,   no.   Oh   God,   we're   gonna

Chorus
G

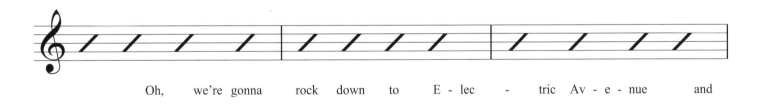

rock   down   to   E - lec - tric Av - e - nue   and   then   we'll   take   it   higher.

Oh,   we're   gonna   rock   down   to   E - lec - tric Av - e - nue   and

then   we'll   take   it   higher.

LOVE ME DO

Words and Music by John Lennon
and Paul McCartney

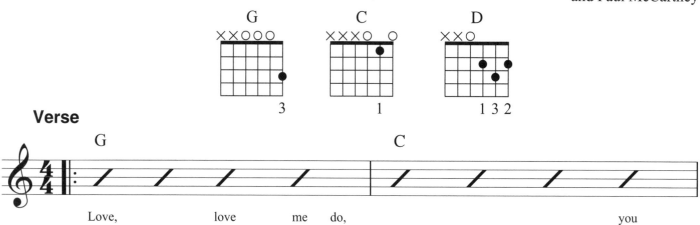

Verse

Love, love me do, you

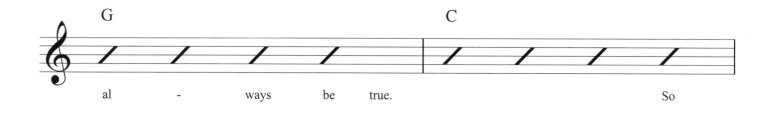

know I love you. I'll

al - ways be true. So

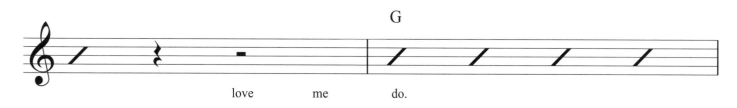

please

love me do.

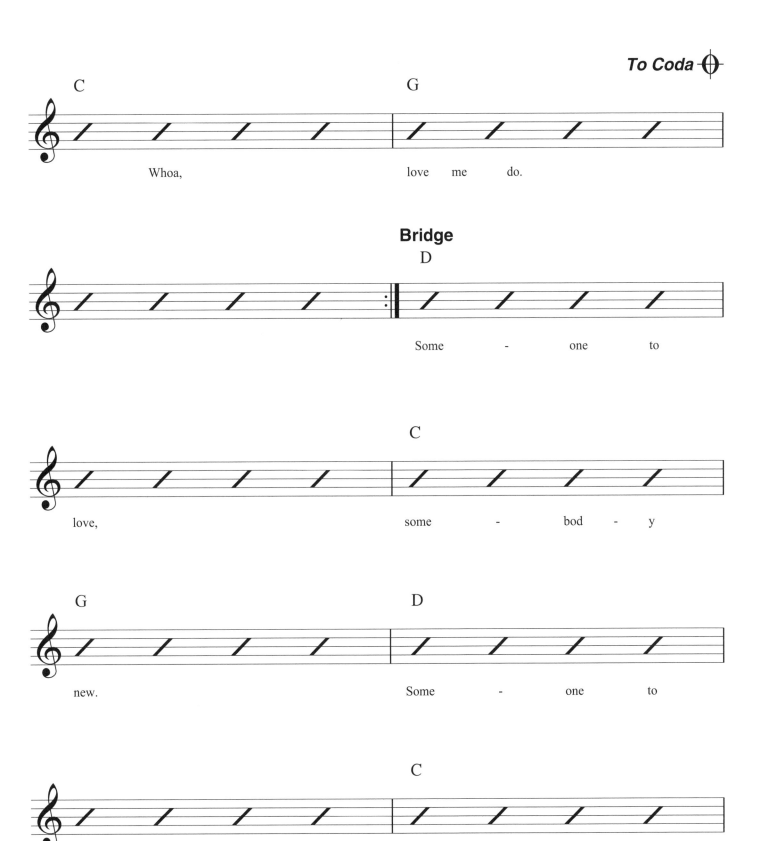

AT THE HOP

Words and Music by Arthur Singer,
John Madara and David White

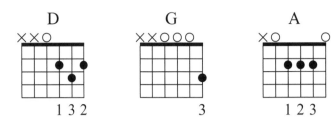

Verse

Well, you can rock it, you can roll it, do the stomp or even stroll it at the

hop.   When the

record starts a spin - nin', you ca - lyp - so when you chicken at the

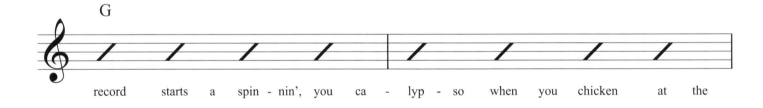

hop.   Do the

dance sen - sa - tion that is sweep - in' the na - tion at the

hop.   Let's   go!

Chorus

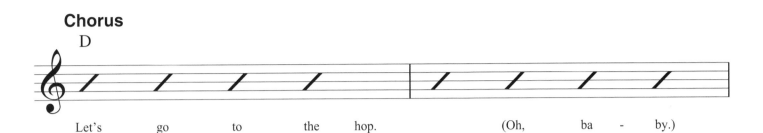

Let's   go   to   the   hop.   (Oh,   ba   -   by.)

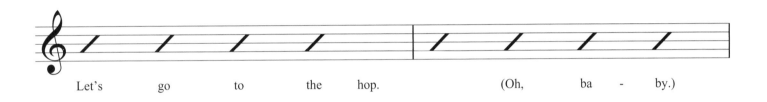

Let's   go   to   the   hop.   (Oh,   ba   -   by.)

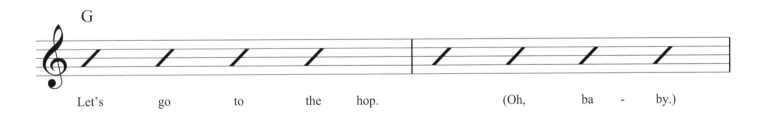

Let's   go   to   the   hop.   (Oh,   ba   -   by.)

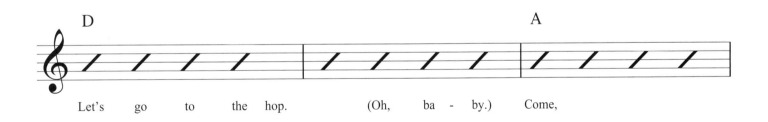

Let's   go   to   the   hop.   (Oh,   ba   -   by.)   Come,

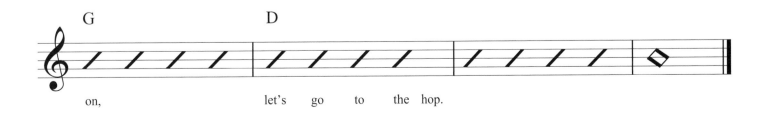

on,   let's   go   to   the   hop.

FLY LIKE AN EAGLE

Words and Music by
Steve Miller

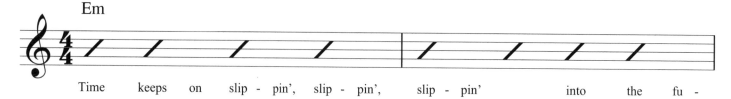

Verse

Time   keeps   on   slip - pin',   slip - pin',   slip - pin'   into   the   fu -

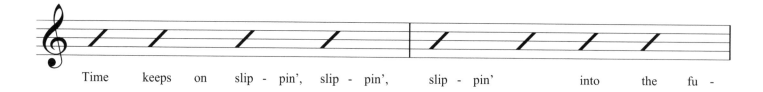

- ture.

Time   keeps   on   slip - pin',   slip - pin',   slip - pin'   into   the   fu -

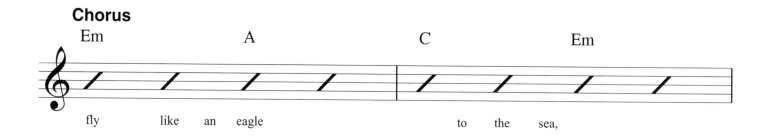

- ture.   I   wanna

Chorus

fly   like   an   eagle   to   the   sea,

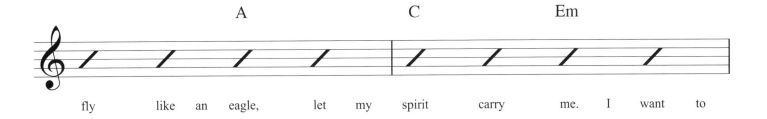

fly   like   an   eagle,   let   my   spirit   carry   me.   I   want   to

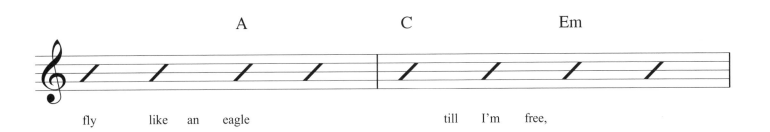

fly   like   an   eagle   till   I'm   free,

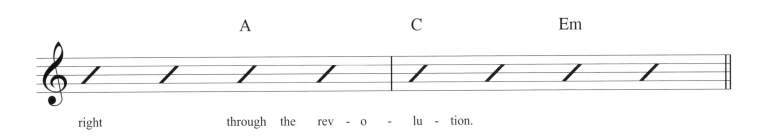

right   through   the   rev - o - lu - tion.

Outro

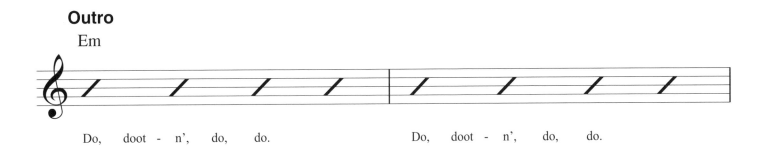

Do,   doot - n',   do,   do.   Do,   doot - n',   do,   do.

Do,   doot - n',   do,   do.

THREE LITTLE BIRDS

Words and Music by
Bob Marley

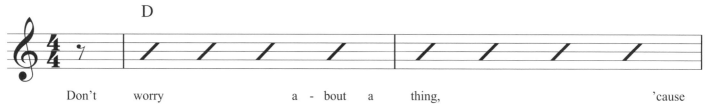

D   G   C   A

𝄋 Chorus

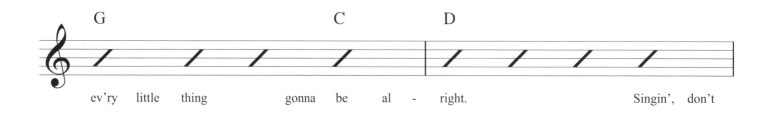

D

Don't   worry   a - bout   a   thing,   'cause

G   C   D

ev'ry   little   thing   gonna   be   al -   right.   Singin',   don't

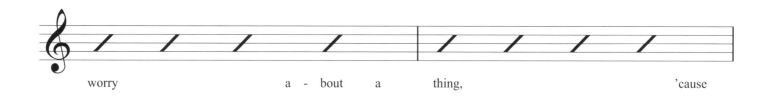

worry   a - bout   a   thing,   'cause

To Coda ⊕

G   C   D

ev'ry   little   thing   gonna   be   al -   right.   Rise   up   this

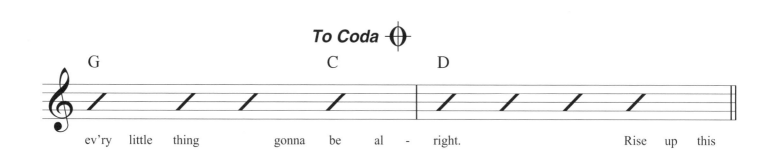

Verse

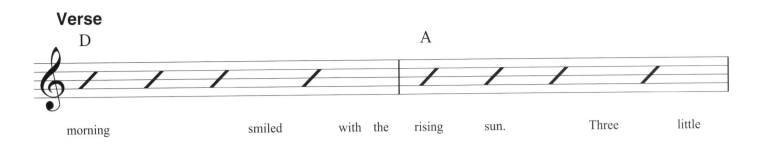

morning   smiled   with   the   rising   sun.   Three   little

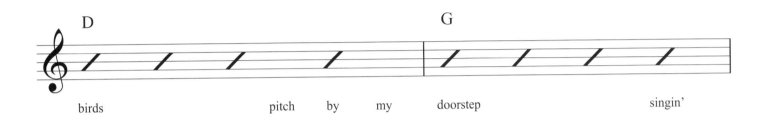

birds   pitch   by   my   doorstep   singin'

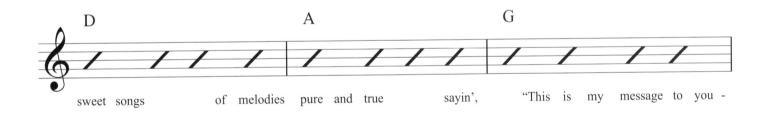

sweet   songs   of   melodies   pure   and   true   sayin',   "This   is   my   message   to   you -

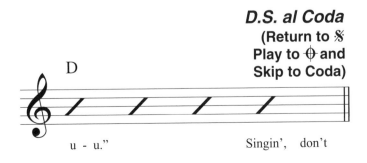

u - u."   Singin',   don't

right.

EVERY BREATH YOU TAKE

Music and Lyrics by Sting

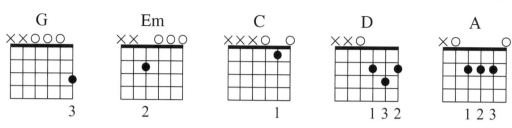

Verse

Ev'ry breath you take,   ev'ry move you
day,   ev'ry word you

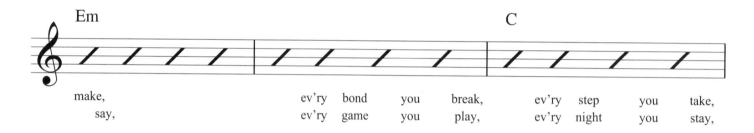

make,   ev'ry bond you break,   ev'ry step you take,
say,   ev'ry game you play,   ev'ry night you stay,

1.

2nd time, skip 1st ending and take 2nd ending

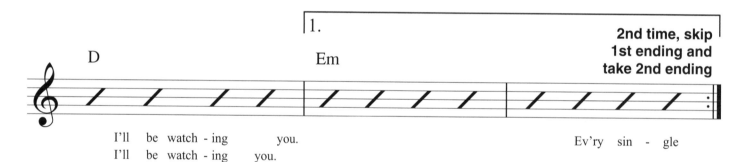

I'll be watch - ing you.   Ev'ry sin - gle
I'll be watch - ing you.

2.

Bridge

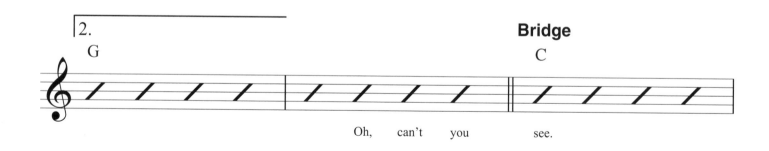

Oh, can't you see.

you be - long to me.   How my poor heart

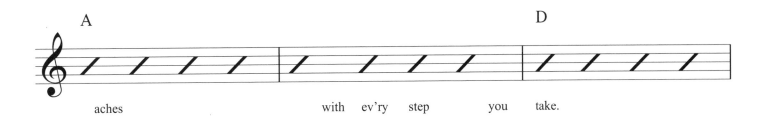

A   D

aches   with ev'ry step   you   take.

Verse

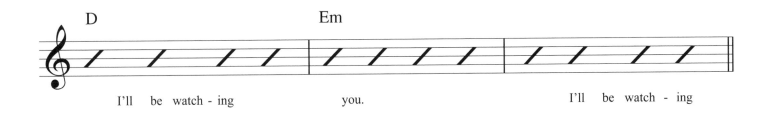

G

Ev'ry move you   make,   ev'ry vow   you

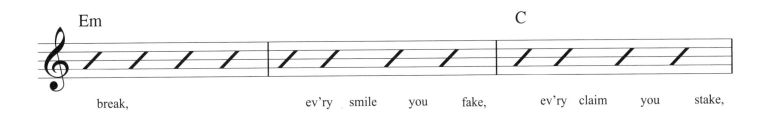

Em   C

break,   ev'ry smile you fake,   ev'ry claim you stake,

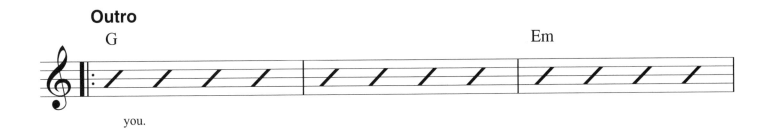

D   Em

I'll be watch - ing   you.   I'll be watch - ing

Outro

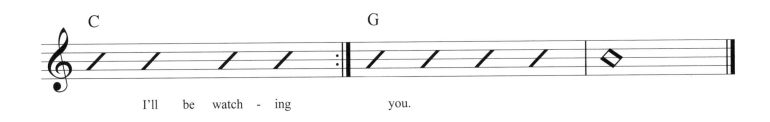

G   Em

you.

C   G

I'll be watch - ing   you.

HAL LEONARD GUITAR METHOD

THE HAL LEONARD GUITAR METHOD is designed for anyone just learning to play acoustic or electric guitar. It is based on years of teaching guitar students of all ages, and it also reflects some of the best guitar teaching ideas from around the world. This comprehensive method includes: A learning sequence carefully paced with clear instructions; popular songs which increase the incentive to learn to play; versatility – can be used as self-instruction or with a teacher; audio accompaniments so that students have fun and sound great while practicing.

BOOK 1

Book 1 provides beginning instruction which includes tuning, playing position, musical symbols, notes in first position, the C, G, G7, D, D7, A7, and Em chords, rhythms through eighth notes, strumming and picking, 100 great songs, riffs, and examples. Includes a chord chart and well-known songs: Ode to Joy • Rockin' Robin • Greensleeves • Give My Regards to Broadway • Time Is on My Side.

00699010 Book $6.99
00699027 Book/CD Pack $10.95

BOOK 2

Book 2 continues the instruction started in Book 1 and covers: Am, Dm, A, E, F and B7 chords; power chords; finger-style guitar; syncopations, dotted rhythms, and triplets; Carter style solos; bass runs; pentatonic scales; improvising; tablature; 92 great songs, riffs and examples; notes in first and second position; and more! The CD includes 57 full-band tracks.

00699020 Book $6.99
00697313 Book/CD Pack $9.95

BOOK 3

Book 3 covers: the major, minor, pentatonic, and chromatic scales, sixteenth notes; barre chords; drop D tuning; movable scales; notes in fifth position; slides, hammer-ons, pull-offs, and string bends; chord construction; gear; 90 great songs, riffs, and examples; and more! The CD includes 61 full-band tracks.

00699030 Book $6.95
00697316 Book/CD Pack $9.95

COMPOSITE

Books 1, 2, and 3 bound together in an easy-to-use spiral binding.

00699040 Books Only $14.95
00697342 Book/3-CD Pack $22.95

VIDEO AND DVD

For the Beginning Electric or Acoustic Guitarist

00697318 DVD $19.95
00320159 VHS Video $14.95
00697341 Book/CD Pack and DVD $24.95

SONGBOOKS

EASY POP RHYTHMS
00697336 Book $6.95
00697309 Book/CD Pack $14.95

MORE EASY POP RHYTHMS
00697338 Book $6.95
00697322 Book/CD Pack....................................$14.95

EVEN MORE EASY POP RHYTHMS
00697340 Book $6.95
00697323 Book/CD Pack $14.95

EASY POP MELODIES
Play along with your favorite hits from the Beatles, Elton John, Elvis Presley, the Police, Nirvana, and more!
00697281 Book $6.95
00697268 Book/CD Pack $14.95

MORE EASY POP MELODIES
00697280 Book $6.95
00697269 Book/CD Pack $14.95

EVEN MORE EASY POP MELODIES
00699154 Book $6.95
00697270 Book/CD Pack $14.95

LEAD LICKS
Over 200 licks in all styles.
00697345 Book/CD Pack......................................$9.95

RHYTHM RIFFS
Over 200 riffs in all styles.
00697346 Book/CD Pack......................................$9.95

STYLISTIC METHODS

ACOUSTIC GUITAR
by Chad Johnson
00697347 Book/CD Pack $16.95

BLUES GUITAR
by Greg Koch
00697326 Book/CD Pack $16.95

CHRISTIAN GUITAR
by Chad Johnson
00695947 Book/CD Pack $12.95

CLASSICAL GUITAR
by Paul Henry
00697376 Book/CD Pack...................................$14.95

COUNTRY GUITAR
by Greg Koch
00697337 Book/CD Pack $22.99

FINGERSTYLE GUITAR
by Chad Johnson
00697378 Book/CD Pack...................................$14.95

FLAMENCO GUITAR
by Hugh Burns
00697363 Book/CD Pack $14.99

JAZZ GUITAR
by Jeff Schroedl
00695359 Book/CD Pack...................................$19.95

ROCK GUITAR
by Michael Mueller
00697319 Book/CD Pack.....................................$16.95

R&B GUITAR
by Dave Rubin
00697356 Book/CD Pack.....................................$14.95

REFERENCE

ARPEGGIO FINDER
An Easy-to-Use Guide to Over 1,300 Guitar Arpeggios
00697352 6" x 9" Edition $5.99
00697351 9" x 12" Edition $6.99

INCREDIBLE CHORD FINDER
An Easy-to-Use Guide to Over 1,100 Guitar Chords
00697200 6" x 9" Edition $5.99
00697208 9" x 12" Edition $6.99

INCREDIBLE SCALE FINDER
An Easy-to-Use Guide to Over 1,300 Guitar Scales
00695568 6" x 9" Edition $5.99
00695490 9" x 12" Edition $6.99

PAPERBACK LESSONS – HAL LEONARD GUITAR METHOD
by Will Schmid and Greg Koch
All three volumes of the world-famous Hal Leonard Guitar Method are now available in one convenient paperback-sized edition, 4-1/4" x 6-3/4"!
00240326 ....$7.95

Prices, contents and availability subject to change without notice.

For More Information, See Your Local Music Dealer, or Write To:

7777 W. Bluemound Rd. P.O. Box 13819 Milwaukee, WI 53213

www.halleonard.com

0609

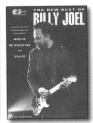

EASY GUITAR WITH NOTES & TAB

This series features simplified arrangements with notes, tab, chord charts, and strum and pick patterns.

MIXED FOLIOS

00702002	Acoustic Rock Hits for Easy Guitar	$12.95
00702166	All-Time Best Guitar Collection	$17.95
00699665	Beatles Best	$12.95
00702232	Best Acoustic Songs for Easy Guitar	$12.99
00702233	Best Hard Rock Songs	$14.99
00698978	Big Christmas Collection	$16.95
00702115	Blues Classics	$10.95
00385020	Broadway Songs for Kids	$9.95
00702237	Christian Acoustic Favorites	$12.95
00702149	Children's Christian Songbook	$7.95
00702028	Christmas Classics	$7.95
00702185	Christmas Hits	$9.95
00702016	Classic Blues for Easy Guitar	$12.95
00702141	Classic Rock	$8.95
00702203	CMT's 100 Greatest Country Songs	$27.95
00702170	Contemporary Christian Christmas	$9.95
00702006	Contemporary Christian Favorites	$9.95
00702065	Contemporary Women of Country	$9.95
00702121	Country from the Heart	$9.95
00702240	Country Hits of 2007-2008	$12.95
00702225	Country Hits of '06-'07	$12.95
00702085	Disney Movie Hits	$12.95
00702257	Easy Acoustic Guitar Songs	$14.99
00702212	Essential Christmas	$9.95
00702041	Favorite Hymns for Easy Guitar	$9.95
00702174	God Bless America®	
	& Other Songs for a Better Nation	$8.95
00699374	Gospel Favorites	$14.95
00702160	The Great American Country Songbook	$12.95
00702050	Great Classical Themes for Easy Guitar	$6.95
00702131	Great Country Hits of the '90s	$8.95
00702116	Greatest Hymns for Guitar	$8.95
00702130	The Groovy Years	$9.95
00702184	Guitar Instrumentals	$9.95
00702231	High School Musical for Easy Guitar	$12.95
00702241	High School Musical 2	$12.95
00702249	High School Musical 3	$12.99
00702037	Hits of the '50s for Easy Guitar	$10.95
00702046	Hits of the '70s for Easy Guitar	$8.95
00702047	Hits of the '80s for Easy Guitar	$9.95
00702032	International Songs for Easy Guitar	$12.95
00702051	Jock Rock for Easy Guitar	$9.95
00702162	Jumbo Easy Guitar Songbook	$19.95
00702112	Latin Favorites	$9.95
00702258	Legends of Rock	$14.99
00702138	Mellow Rock Hits	$10.95
00702147	Motown's Greatest Hits	$9.95
00702114	Movie Love Songs	$9.95
00702039	Movie Themes	$10.95
00702210	Best of MTV Unplugged	$12.95
00702189	MTV's 100 Greatest Pop Songs	$24.95
00702187	Selections from *O Brother Where Art Thou?*	$12.95
00702178	100 Songs for Kids	$12.95
00702158	Songs from Passion	$9.95
00702125	Praise and Worship for Guitar	$9.95
00702155	Rock Hits for Guitar	$9.95
00702242	Rock Band	$19.95
00702256	Rock Band 2	$19.99
00702128	Rockin' Down the Highway	$9.95
00702207	Smash Hits for Guitar	$9.95
00702110	The Sound of Music	$9.99
00702124	Today's Christian Rock – 2nd Edition	$9.95
00702220	Today's Country Hits	$9.95
00702198	Today's Hits for Guitar	$9.95
00702217	Top Christian Hits	$12.95
00702235	Top Christian Hits of '07-'08	$14.95
00702246	Top Hits of 2008	$12.95
00702206	Very Best of Rock	$9.95
00702175	VH1's 100 Greatest Songs of Rock and Roll	$24.95
00702192	Worship Favorites	$9.95

ARTIST COLLECTIONS

00702001	Best of Aerosmith	$16.95
00702040	Best of the Allman Brothers	$12.95
00702169	Best of The Beach Boys	$10.95
00702201	The Essential Black Sabbath	$12.95
00702140	Best of Brooks & Dunn	$10.95
00702095	Best of Mariah Carey	$12.95
00702043	Best of Johnny Cash	$12.95
00702033	Best of Steven Curtis Chapman	$14.95
00702073	Steven Curtis Chapman – Favorites	$10.95
00702090	Eric Clapton's Best	$10.95
00702086	Eric Clapton – from the Album *Unplugged*	$10.95
00702202	The Essential Eric Clapton	$12.95
00702250	blink-182 – Greatest Hits	$12.99
00702053	Best of Patsy Cline	$10.95
00702229	The Very Best of Creedence Clearwater Revival	$12.95
00702145	Best of Jim Croce	$10.95
00702219	David Crowder*Band Collection	$12.95
00702122	The Doors for Easy Guitar	$12.99
00702099	Best of Amy Grant	$9.95
00702190	Best of Pat Green	$19.95
00702136	Best of Merle Haggard	$10.95
00702243	Hannah Montana	$14.95
00702244	Hannah Montana 2/Meet Miley Cyrus	$16.95
00702227	Jimi Hendrix – Smash Hits	$14.99
00702236	Best of Antonio Carlos Jobim	$12.95
00702087	Best of Billy Joel	$10.95
00702245	Elton John – Greatest Hits 1970-2002	$14.99
00702204	Robert Johnson	$9.95
00702199	Norah Jones – Come Away with Me	$10.95
00702234	Selections from Toby Keith – 35 Biggest Hits	$12.95
00702003	Kiss	$9.95
00702193	Best of Jennifer Knapp	$12.95
00702097	John Lennon – Imagine	$9.95
00702216	Lynyrd Skynyrd	$14.95
00702182	The Essential Bob Marley	$12.95
00702129	Songs of Sarah McLachlan	$12.95
02501316	Metallica – Death Magnetic	$15.95
00702209	Steve Miller Band –	
	Young Hearts (Greatest Hits)	$12.95
00702096	Best of Nirvana	$14.95
00702211	The Offspring – Greatest Hits	$12.95
00702030	Best of Roy Orbison	$12.95
00702144	Best of Ozzy Osbourne	$12.95
00702139	Elvis Country Favorites	$9.95
00699415	Best of Queen for Guitar	$14.99
00702208	Red Hot Chili Peppers – Greatest Hits	$12.95
00702093	Rolling Stones Collection	$17.95
00702092	Best of the Rolling Stones	$14.99
00702196	Best of Bob Seger	$12.95
00702252	Frank Sinatra – Nothing But the Best	$12.99
00702010	Best of Rod Stewart	$14.95
00702150	Best of Sting	$12.95
00702049	Best of George Strait	$12.95
00702259	Taylor Swift for Easy Guitar	$12.99
00702223	Chris Tomlin – Arriving	$12.95
00702226	Chris Tomlin – See the Morning	$12.95
00702132	Shania Twain – Greatest Hits	$10.95
00702108	Best of Stevie Ray Vaughan	$10.95
00702123	Best of Hank Williams	$9.95
00702111	Stevie Wonder – Guitar Collection	$9.95
00702228	Neil Young – Greatest Hits	$12.99
00702188	Essential ZZ Top	$10.95

Prices, contents and availability subject to change without notice.

0709

E-Z PLAY® GUITAR

EASY TO READ NOTES WITH TABLATURE

*This series features your favorite songs in easy-to-play arrangements. The easy-to-read E-Z Play notes name themselves, while the TAB notation tells you where to play the notes on the guitar. The arrangements can be played solo or as a duet using the Strum and Picking patterns. E-Z Play Guitar books can be used to supplement **any guitar method** Book 1!*

BEATLES CLASSIC HITS

18 great songs from the Fab Four: Drive My Car • Get Back • Help! • I Saw Her Standing There • If I Fell • Love Me Do • Nowhere Man • Revolution • Twist and Shout • We Can Work It Out • more.
00702019 ....$12.99

BEATLES GREATEST HITS

19 songs: Can't Buy Me Love • Eleanor Rigby • A Hard Day's Night • Hey Jude • Let It Be • Penny Lane • She Loves You • Ticket to Ride • Yesterday • and more.
00702072 ....$9.95

CHRISTMAS TIDINGS

23 Christmas favorites, including: Blue Christmas • The Chipmunk Song • Feliz Navidad • Grandma Got Run Over by a Reindeer • Happy Holiday • I'll Be Home for Christmas • Rudolph the Red-Nosed Reindeer • Silver Bells • and more.
00699123 ....$10.99

CLASSIC ROCK FOR GUITAR

16 songs, including: All Right Now • Angie • Born to Be Wild • Free Bird • Iron Man • My Generation • Nights in White Satin • Rock and Roll All Nite • and more.
00702036...$9.95

CLASSICAL THEMES

20 beloved classical themes: Air on the G String • Ave Maria • Für Elise • In the Hall of the Mountain King • Jesu, Joy of Man's Desiring • Largo • Ode to Joy • Pomp and Circumstance • and more. Ideal for beginning or vision-impaired players.
00699272...$9.95

COUNTRY FAVORITES

20 songs, including: Green Green Grass of Home • Hey, Good Lookin' • Jambalaya (On the Bayou) • Make the World Go Away • Your Cheatin' Heart • and more.
00702077 ....$8.95

THE CREAM OF CLAPTON

19 hits from his early years, including: Crossroads • I Shot the Sheriff • Knockin' on Heaven's Door • Layla • White Room • Wonderful Tonight • and more.
00702024 ....$10.95

THE DOORS

Features 16 of The Doors' greatest hits, including: Break on Through (To the Other Side) • Crystal Ship • Five to One • Hello, I Love You • L.A. Woman • Light My Fire • Love Her Madly • Love Me Two Times • People Are Strange • Riders on the Storm • Touch Me • Twentieth Century Fox • more.
00699176...$9.95

FAVORITE CHILDREN'S SONGS

28 songs: The Alphabet Song • The Farmer in the Dell • Jack and Jill • Oh, Susanna • Old MacDonald Had a Farm • This Old Man • Three Blind Mice • and more.
00702079 ....$8.95

GLORIOUS HYMNS

30 inspirational hymns: Abide with Me • Amazing Grace • Blessed Assurance • Come Christians Join to Sing • In the Garden • Jacob's Ladder • Rock of Ages • What a Friend We Have in Jesus • Wondrous Love • more.
00699192 ....$9.95

GOSPEL SONGS TO LIVE BY

20 songs, including: Amazing Grace • At Calvary • At the Cross • Blessed Assurance • Count Your Blessings • Do Lord • Footsteps of Jesus • Higher Ground • I Surrender All • Just as I Am • O Happy Day • Rock of Ages • This Little Light of Mine • What a Friend We Have in Jesus • more.
00699236...$7.95

GREAT ACOUSTIC HITS

Features 15 of the best acoustic songs: Barely Breathing • Best of My Love • Blackbird • Dust in the Wind • Fast Car • Love Song • Mr. Jones • Name • Only Wanna Be with You • Patience • Silent Lucidity • Tears in Heaven • Wanted Dead or Alive • Wonderwall • You Were Meant for Me.
00699127 ....$9.99

KIDS' GUITAR SONGBOOK

A big collection of 38 favorites: Alphabet Song • A Bicycle Built for Two • Bingo • Eensy Weensy Spider • The Farmer in the Dell • Home on the Range • Jesus Loves Me • Old MacDonald • Sailing, Sailing • Twinkle, Twinkle Little Star • Yankee Doodle • more.
00702102 ....$8.95

OLD TIME GOSPEL SONGS

23 songs, including: Amazing Grace • Because He Lives • How Great Thou Art • Just a Closer Walk with Thee • (There'll Be) Peace in the Valley (For Me) • Rock of Ages • Sweet By and By • Will the Circle Be Unbroken • and more.
00702022...$9.95

THE BEST OF ELVIS PRESLEY

18 of the King's best, including: All Shook Up • Blue Suede Shoes • Hound Dog • Heartbreak Hotel • (Let Me Be Your) Teddy Bear • and more.
00702083...$9.95

SUNDAY SCHOOL SONGS

31 wonderful songs of inspiration, including: Amazing Grace • The B-I-B-L-E • Deep and Wide • Go Tell It on the Mountain • Hallelu, Hallelujah! • I Am a C-H-R-I-S-T-I-A-N • Jesus Loves Me • Kum Ba Yah • This Little Light of Mine • and more.
00699220...$7.95

25 CHRISTMAS FAVORITES

25 songs: Away in a Manger • The Conventry Carol • Deck the Hall • Jolly Old St. Nicholas • Joy to the World • Up on the Housetop • and more.
00702075...$10.95

For more information contact your local music dealer or contact:

HAL•LEONARD® CORPORATION
7777 W. BLUEMOUND RD. P.O. BOX 13819 MILWAUKEE, WI 53213

www.halleonard.com

Prices, availability and contents subject to change without notice.